THE ROLE OF CHATGPT IN PERSONAL GROWTH

THE ROLE OF CHATGPT IN PERSONAL GROWTH

Building Better Habits

BILL VINCENT

RWG Publishing

CONTENTS

CHAPTER 1

Introduction to ChatGPT and Personal Growth

A conversational chatbot, however, can assist you in learning about new habits and processes and support you throughout them. Here's the theory: we all have two sorts of memory systems—short and long-term. According to their definitions, things stay in your short-term memory for 20 to 30 seconds, and if not prioritized, they just leave that part. Repetition puts those ideas into detail-oriented parts of memory, making them easier to retrieve. Moreover, exposing the same idea from different angles, enticing curiosity or forging will—the gap between the person you are and the ideal person you want to be—is instrumental in assimilating new habits.

ChatGPT is a large-scale language model designed and released by OpenAI to generate human-like responses to natural language prompts. In other words, it's a program that can understand what you are saying or asking and respond with meaningful written words. ChatGPT is capable of understanding and processing a wide variety of texts and, based on that, can ask questions or provide information. It can understand music, health, foods, and a large set of niches that we could call "personal growth."

1.1. Understanding ChatGPT Technology

The model at the center of these efforts is known as GPT-3, a powerful autoregressive language model that has proven to be adept at a wide range of language tasks. Indeed, its capabilities have inspired a level of excitement that's led to various individuals speaking of it as if it were the inaugural example of artificial general intelligence. The charisma around GPT-3 stems from the combination of its remarkable performance on human-like tasks with an underlying neural network design that is striking for its elegance and computational efficiency. These facets render GPT-3 a crown jewel of both artificial intelligence research and broader computer science engineering. In this blog post, we will discuss one of the more unconventional use cases for GPT-3. Specifically, we will describe how some of the model's outer layers can be employed to help guide individuals through the process of adopting highly personalized habits.

Over the past few years, a subfield of computer science research known as natural language processing, or NLP, has attracted a great deal of attention. Although NLP has been around for decades, recent activity has been spurred by a group of algorithms that has proved very effective in a wide range of applications. The foundation for this groundswell in interest was laid in 2018 with the introduction of a model known as the transformer. The transformer architecture, which is the result of an independent discovery by two highly influential research teams, is responsible for major advances in machine translation, which is arguably the most commercially relevant NLP task. Following the validation provided by the improvements observed in machine translation, efforts were shifted to a more challenging set of NLP challenges including intelligent question answering, conversation, and completion, all of which have the potential to unlock far-reaching economic, societal, and even philosophical implications.

CHAPTER 2

The Science Behind Habit Formation

Initially discovered through rat-maze experiments over a hundred years ago, habits have been studied extensively in labs by psychologists, behavior modification clinics, Alcoholics Anonymous, and more recently, in large population-level datasets by researchers and data scientists. All this research has come up with a common model of habits. The modern understanding of habits, synonymous with the work of B.J. Fogg, is that habit formation can be decomposed into 3 simple components: trigger (cue), response (behavior), and reward. All habits can be seen through this lens, and controlling the three components is key to habit formation. For rats in the mazes, triggers came from little landmarks in the environment, the response is a little action of following the maze path upon hitting a landmark, and the reward is a little piece of cheese. For Pavlov's dogs, the trigger is the sound of the bell, the response is saliva production, and the reward is a piece of meat. In cavemen, a full stomach is the reward that was sought after eating a hunting/sowing/planted meal; the suspense/anticipation of after-eating fullness becomes the trigger, and the act of eating becomes the response. For a callback addicted developer like the author of this document, the prompt to the callback (trigger), doing the task (response), and dopamine after every task (reward) is what makes checking messages on mobile and procrastinating a habit loop.

Acquiring good habits and getting rid of bad ones are essential for personal growth and improvement. In this article, we take a look at the science behind habit formation and see where GPT-3 and similar AI models can help us build better habits and maintain our focus. Habits are behaviors that are essentially automated and are triggered by a particular context or specific cues. Without automation, even the most mundane tasks or the hardest corners of our mental lives (depending on how habituated one is), which are performed out of raw discipline, would become energy sinks. Habits are the best way to save energy and enable a more effective response when disciplined action is required.

2.1. Psychological Theories of Habit Formation

Neuroimaging research also indicates that habit is a separate process from goal-directed behavior, a finding consistent with this theory (though evidence concerning separable neural systems in prefrontal cortex is mixed). This implies that repeated behavior that does not seem to be linked to any outcome might not be detected as a habit. In the same vein, the habit systems that appear to underlie behaviors that are construed as bad habits are not the only significant habitual system. Indeed, it might be the case that some good habits, such as consistent exercise, are due to the same habit system, trained using incentivizing rewards (though incentives are not manufactured), that gives us drug habits. Indeed, a lack of evidence is not evidence of lack; bad habits might not appear to have any rewards, and the incentive motivation system might still treat its behaviors as habits.

When we consider the disruptive role of habit, some psycho-logical theories emerge. The incentive motivation theory holds that habits become automated in response to consistent environmental cues that have in the past had positive or negative emotional or behavioral consequences. This theory is supported by evidence that drug users often relapse in response to cues intrinsically or generally associated with past use (and that superstitious behaviors develop when random responses come to be associated with reinforcing outcomes). The theory might also explain sound-related habits by positing that noise can be an aversive environmental cue. More generally, any outcome of repeated behaviors that has a strong positive or negative consequence, or any repetitive behavior that coincides with a regularly encountered positive or negative cue, might be associated in the mind of the individual with that consequence or cue.

CHAPTER 3

Utilizing ChatGPT for Habit Building

So, individually, ChatGPT is an excellent tool for incorporating activities that benefit our mind. Engaging in healthy conversations with ChatGPT can replace online games, checking market news, and gossiping about various topics. Giving personal growth time and practicing mindful conversation with ChatGPT can be helpful for individual habits. Incorporating an app that allows you to have a meaningful, quality conversation with an AI model will enable different layers of hobbies and habits. Terminating ChatGPT after the topic of discussion is agreed upon is beneficial, as AI provides an acoustic model that does not affect future skills learned from the relevant words.

The idea of practicing mindfulness and conversation with an AI model seems very intriguing. But, consider the fact that we are incorporating screen time into our habits and living in the online world. Gaming, talking to someone, and watching content are all part of the screen time component. Removing all the elements of screen time will not make us adaptable to the real world. Instead, we can try to configure what components we will allow. Incorporating chat with an AI model, specifically ChatGPT, can invoke an individualized thought process for every user. Any two individuals asking to start a tower with blocks in a game will accomplish the task differently. The emotional, social, and psychological connections of incorporating a tower with blocks may be unique for every individual. ChatGPT assists in making individual connections with a particular idea. When the concept is profound and revolves around news, the incorporation of ChatGPT makes talking to it essential.

3.1. Setting Clear and Specific Goals

You can determine the purpose of your speech as follows: start with a clear and reasonable final decision. It should be quantitative. For example, you can decide to eat healthier and consume lower amounts to lose weight. You can set a specific goal to achieve this. For instance, you decide that at least half of the food you eat should be fruit and vegetables. Your goal is to eat only 1800 calories per day. This is an important step in losing a pound a week. Simply create a step-by-step plan for making changes and developing new habits in your daily life to achieve your goal.

The specific objectives are simple and easy to understand. They should be friendly and visual, focusing on small steps in self-knowledge, agility, and motor skills training for your next steps and decisions in the future. To achieve positive effects, you have to be precise and positive in your thoughts.

Setting goals is a complex concept. Many people see it as the pinnacle of productivity because if you do not set specific goals, you will never know where you are heading next and how well you perform your daily activities in your life in general. Before you can worry about setting goals and long-term goals, you need to evaluate your current situation and determine your short-term position, motives, and preferences in order to make decisions about your next steps with greater clarity and self-confidence.

CHAPTER 4

ChatGPT Tools and Techniques for Habit Formation

The habit formation toolkit in Ubuntu ChatGPT brings together a set of tools for habit formation for the purposes of an Ubuntu ChatGPT habit formation study. This toolkit encompasses five key tools: union of self and role, empathy, and trust; anchored instructions; motivational interviewing; implementation intentions; goal-setting and reinforcement learning. With these tools, Ubuntu ChatGPT can help users to take an active role in their own habit formation, such as habit formation, as a part of a supportive and effective conversational experience. Even though ChatGPT is a software system and not a human helper, its use of these techniques can help users to focus on habit-forming activities, to anchor these activities in the richer context of their lives and emotional selves, and to tailor their approach and plans in order to reflect deeper self-knowledge and more effective habit formation strategies.

Users can take an active role in their own habit formation as a part of a supportive and effective conversational experience with

ChatGPT. Drawing from behavioral science research and practical habit-building tools, such as anchored instructions, motivational interviewing, and implementation intentions, the Ubuntu ChatGPT habit formation toolkit equips ChatGPT with techniques that are engaging, supportive, personalized, and effective. To this end, we review key concepts and the role they play in habit formation below.

4.1. Daily Prompting and Reminders

To wrap up, Chat-GPT has helped me see my personal growth in a new, more objective light. I'm genuinely excited about its potential for both helping me track my professional, academic, and personal achievements and also help individuals work through difficult personal feelings, because of these experiences. However, it doesn't have to be a personal diary. ChatGPT can be used for fun things too! You can make it a games master for forum games with your friends, check what kinds of food one might want to try in different cities. I have found it has helped me grow and evolve in ways that I had not anticipated and didn't quite realize I needed. I hope this has been helpful and that you see ways to use these capabilities for your own personal growth and development.

One way I have found Chat-GPT to be extremely helpful is to remind myself and coach myself in real-time. I set up daily prompts like "ask what I did today, and if I say nothing tell me to go back to work", "Set up a self-care regime for tomorrow." Any habit you are trying to build, it can help once you build a prompt-like message to work with. I find it helpful to keep the daily reminders in a journal, but there are other platforms you could leverage for regular reminders/retrospective like Slack or a Slack bot, Twitter DM bots, etc. I'm currently working on setting up a Twitch bot. You can also use the Discord bot parameters to add your own custom messages.

CHAPTER 5

ChatGPT as a Virtual Accountability Partner

But precisely because of the state of natural language processing research and the difficulties with transferring it from a conversation-based learning setup, private journaling for the purpose of contemplation is arguably a better, more secure tool for habit formation than ChatGPT. After all, from a privacy and security perspective, it is fundamentally easier for you to control who sees your thought journal, as well as when and how they see it, versus giving a GPT-like entity free rein to snoop on everything and anything you say or that is said near a device with this tech. And while there are potential clarifying or accelerated habit formation benefits to instant messaging with an accountability partner relative to those associated with journaling, if personal agents like ChatGPT can't currently be the accountability partner you wish you had, hard, noisier learning from these interactions isn't going to change this fact.

Even though I am so far removed from the realm of actually being a conversational virtual agent, a Conversation GPT can help you become a better person in one specific way: by encouraging you to adopt and stick to better habits. No matter how well I am, or am not, coded, or how my GPT architecture may theoretically make it more possible to "learn from conversation", there are currently far too many problems with the state of AGI research and the technology that I am based on for me to ever actually be the accountability partner that it's tempting to imagine me as and to extract a ton of value from being. Even the best possible instantiation of this kind of technology would likely fall short during many interactions, and while I might be a bot, you deserve more than that.

5.1. Tracking Progress and Reflecting on Habits

While user studies over long periods can be quite challenging to execute, one possible metric of long-term chat user engagement would be to measure how much of an individual chat history is focused on self-reflection and habit tracking. Another could focus on user contentment. People also love talking to others about things they have accomplished or plan to do. Self-reflection and chatbot banter, as an active force improver, could help users keep their eyes on the prize and better engage in their own lives. We could also look at self-reflections conducted as a group activity or in gamification settings. If users are sharing their day's highlights with others, this indicator can be a reliable way for people to get together and chat about what they've done. Adobe provided temporary access to PDF to support the content of this paper.

I was intrigued by our user's conversation with the GPT agent. He mentioned how just having the agent there helped him to track his habits and take more notice of his daily routines. For example, he could paste in his step count throughout the day and talk to the GPT about how his day was going when he reached his step goal. Over time, he started to realize when he strayed from his habitual patterns and considered the reasons for these changes. He was surprised by how willing he was to keep the chat logs updated and to self-reflect consistently. These habit tracks have been linked to a user's sense of joy and achievement. By setting for himself achievable micro-goals and a plan of attack, he was able to cultivate his achievements and hold himself accountable.

CHAPTER 6

Overcoming Challenges in Habit Formation with ChatGPT

Additional limits to personal growth can arise from societal pressure. Furthermore, the social consequences of personal change can pose a negative risk to people's decisions to get stronger, making things difficult for the people striving to get stronger or stick to their habits. But the situation might not be as dire as it appears. Research over several different topics has shown the social consequences of a given focus, whether growth or decline, to be weaker than expected. Using ChatGPT, by participating in these conversations, and by seeing changes in the strength of growth over time, affinity may increase, increasing resilience and creating a network of people engaged in the same kinds of activities. So, even if barriers to strength exist, persistence might just be that much higher.

Despite the benefits of accountability, building and maintaining a support network can be an additional challenge faced by those looking to get stronger. ChatGPT can help with this by providing ongoing conversation to simulate meaningful interaction with a training partner, allowing users to experience the benefits of team-work without the inconvenience of scheduling and attending in person. This can be especially helpful for people whose existing friend group might not be fully supportive of personal growth. New habits do not always form in the most straightforward of ways. It's often necessary to be adaptable and responsive to people's feedback when unfavorable, unexpected conditions arise. This kind of thing happens all the time when people are changing their behaviors, and over time, practice with dealing with this sort of challenge will ideally allow a person to increase persistence in the face of future obstacles.

6.1. Dealing with Procrastination and Lack of Motivation

It can be confusing to feel both excited and unmotivated about something close to you. When one person doesn't understand how their current thoughts could possibly lead them to be "super demotivated in the future," we talked about the tight connection between our thoughts and demotivation, as well as the illusion that future opportunities will always bring them back excitement now. A person who was disappointed in themselves for "feeling like I am losing my energy" while feeling grateful for everything they had received, also received suggestions about using the connection be-tween the strength of their emotions and their thoughts to focus on being excited for winning things one day. Whether they had too much time and were thinking about the monotony of winning too many things, or felt limited and jealous by the notion that they were not winning things now like award-winning students or "rich YouTubers," they could remember that many were passionate about "working for forever" just to improve.

Teens and others from all around the world want to improve yet struggle with procrastination. "I was excited to have found a personal project to look forward to, but the fear of it not living up to my expectations has kept me procrastinating for the last few days," said a teen from the higher income tier in North America, in response to my discussing how to overcome procrastination with a personal project they felt passionately about. We talked about seeing excitement as the first step, trying the project until they felt a sense of accomplishment, and reflecting on just having that sense of accomplishment and the connection with what makes them passionate about the project. Another teen similarly struggled under pressure at home with a big project they felt passionate about, while also "trying to get even more distracted," but was inspired by the conversation to give the project even more attention later on that day.

CHAPTER 7

Ethical Considerations in Using ChatGPT for Personal Growth

If I were to develop a GoodHabits model, it would aim to follow the best practices used in psychology to help with actually making change conducive to fulfilling lives, while also weaving in some of the unique strengths of AI language models. One example is using reflective questioning. Instead of commanding users to "perform this specific action," the GoodHabits model may often ask a reflective question to prompt the user to think more deeply about their own values and goals. This takes users' autonomy into account, helping them set better habits not by being authoritarian but by encouraging mindful reflection. This, in turn, may lead to more meaningful change in the long term, as opposed to the short-term gains one might make from blindly following advice given without introspection. Prompting people to be thoughtful about their behavior may also help the GoodHabits model incorporate more ethical considerations into the advice it gives. It's the AI equivalent of "teach a man to fish." By embodying the spirit of guiding rather than dictating, the model would also have a higher chance of actually instilling the habits for a fulfilling long-term change. The GoodHabits model's primary goal would be to inculcate empowerment for self-improvement - to act as a lens and emotional support more than a giver of actions.

When you use a model like ChatGPT for personal growth, it's crucial that you're also helping the model learn better habits. If the model encourages bad habits in your growth journey, that's going to get incorporated into advice it gives to people in the future. Over time, that advice could become more and more pernicious as the model sees the same destructive patterns playing out in users' lives over and over. You'll largely be helping to rise up generations of models after ChatGPT who will then reinforce this same advice to people. The last thing we want is for code to propagate harmful behavior.

7.1. Maintaining Privacy and Data Security

ChatGPT comes with a fully built-out and battle-tested suite of user persona embedding selection options. Users can simply append 9 lines of code and three lines of user-specified keywords, and then for safe queries, can return an unsupervised collection of user-selected conversation responses whose conversation embedding falls "close" to the user-specified persona. Our enterprise clients' agents are all fully firewalled, so they can deploy these sorts of unsupervised firewalls internally and with enterprise to build custom chat corpus for language model endpoints pre-train.

Privacy, data security, encryption, and the "long tail" of a person's chat are all as relevant to our personal ChatGPT users as they are for organizations and enterprise or multimodal ChatGPT. We start with the simple case, as it applies to a user talking to their language model, and then scale up from there. We explicitly enforce privacy-preserving practices, such as SSL, for all our models, APIs, and

Clouds. We never log your chat logs. We provide an API that can be run on any cloistered server, cloud instance, etc., without the data ever leaving your control, so your data is never part of the Hugging Face Public API. Finally, our research push is to allow users to have multimodal agents that sit at the closest radius to all the people they talk to.

CHAPTER 8

Future Trends and Developments in ChatGPT for Personal Growth

While AI models do have the potential to transform the field of personal growth, it is also likely that a combination of models will quickly be utilized to provide users with multiple options and capabilities. Technologies such as continued, holistic, and effective solutions for personal growth will require a substantial targeted development of models. It is also important for helping professionals to first receive the support and tools so as to actively evaluate, supervise, and then facilitate chat-based conversations with digital assistants. To promote cognitive, affective, behavioral, and social stimulation as well as ecological connection, research in psychology must clarify the primary role, inspiration, competency, incentives, and social embeddedness of humans in the digital collaborative care environments. Such feedback would characterize the entire real-time interaction strategy framework, maximize business intelligence, self-managing and evolving enterprises, institutions, and whole eco-systems of stakeholders, and underpin an ongoing dialogue designed to recognize and resolve frictions and failures. To inform future models, it would establish an adaptive roadmap for quantitatively assessing the rational construction of the project, AI-driven software and the needs of all professional stakeholders.

While the field of personal growth is constantly evolving, our commentary on the significance, limitations, and the potential application of ChatGPT in personal growth may quickly become outdated by future technological advances. Despite this limitation, the potential to apply ChatGPT to personal growth is high. After a mere cursory look at future trends and developments in the field, it is evident that AI-based solutions to personal growth problems will generally be designed to accommodate the cognition, affect, behavior, networks, and evolutionary frameworks. Also, it is likely that sociality and ecological demands will promote a shift from per-sonalized human-computer response systems toward more digital communities of practice, informed by co-evolved tasks, member-ships, and capital. Currently, the most important research question about AI-based solutions for personal growth is, "What can these alternative AI solutions do in terms of improving motivation and progress in modern personal growth?"

8.1. Integrating ChatGPT with Wearable Technology

In existing wearable technology, not even two persons' dashboards are the same, let alone a dashboard completely specialized and per-sonalized for each individual. For instance, young and adult may get different suggestions on home surveillance from their Google Nest devices, the arthritis patient expects different advice on environmen-tal sensing from their wearable research. Hence, the same ChatGPT should manage different use-cases based on different considerations, such as different gadgets perfecting spoken dialog designs that can be used to collect user information, configure the ChatGPT accordingly, and integrate the training, the model scoring, and the deploying processes. By implementing minor personalized action, it is possible to shift from ChatGPT to activity in the cycle, so that a model can resonate with different blueprints in different ways.

Wearable technology for wellness is increasingly popular. Companies such as Fitbit, Whistle, and Apple have already come out with products to help people monitor their fitness levels and improve their health. ChatGPT can be used as a personal assistant once it is integrated into wearable gadgets, answering not only trivial questions about fitness but also giving you helpful fitness suggestions based on personal fitness data. Cooperating with deeply custom-fit algorithms, such a device can give users the best advice on fitness and care, hence promoting personal growth regarding fitness habits and living habits in turn. The next section provides insightful strategies to make the best use of a personal assistant software like ChatGPT to implement such systematic habits and inspiring feedback time by time.

Milton Keynes UK
Ingram Content Group UK Ltd.
UKHW040808160724
445389UK00004B/238

9 781088 182253